Mary Pickford in
Secrets 1933
by Adrian

Deborah Kerr in
The King & I 1956
by Irene Sharaff

Loretta Young
in *Suez* 1938
by Royer

Do not cut
space between
arm & dress

Do not cut
space between
arm & dress

Jennifer Jones in
Madame Bovary 1949
by Walter Plunkett

Do not cut
space between
arm & dress

Paulette Goddard in
Reap the Wild Wind 1942
by Natalie Visart

Jeanette MacDonald in
San Francisco 1936
by Adrian

Do not cut
space between
arm & dress

Marcella Martin in
Gone with the Wind 1939
by Walter Plunkett

Miriam Hopkins in
The Old Maid 1939
by Orry-Kelly

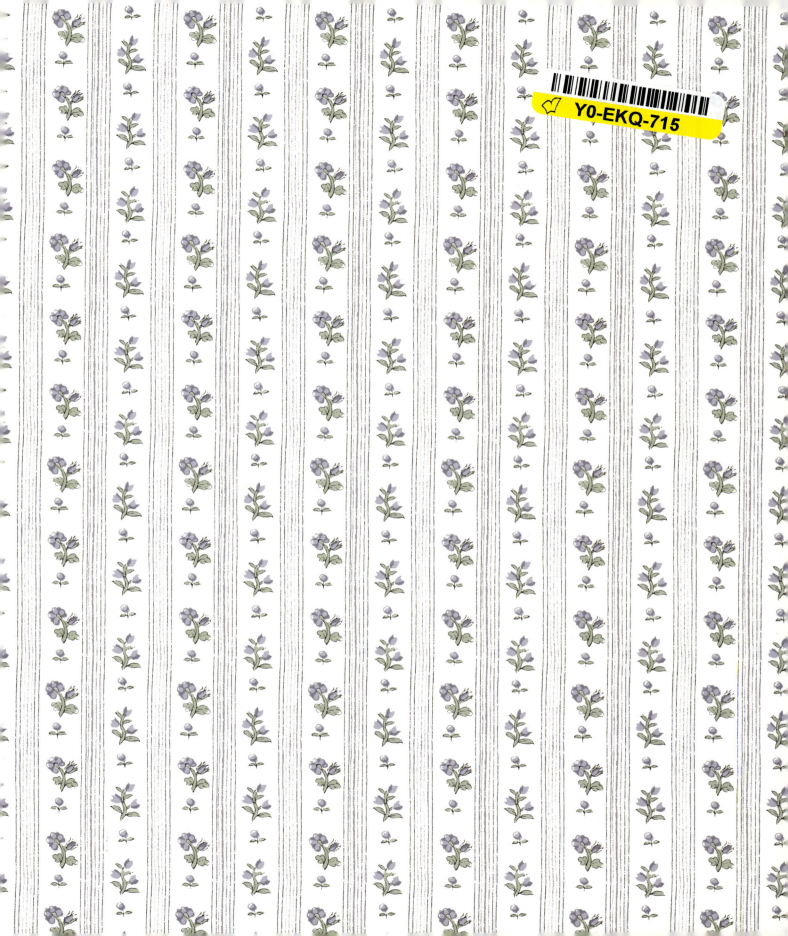

Paper-backed linen in a vintage-inspired print
covers the walls of a powder room designed by
Billy Cotton; the mirror, delicately suspended from
a vintage ribbon, feels almost as if it's floating.

Charm
School

Becky Nielsen transformed a small butler's pantry into a floral oasis, decoupaging walls with pages cut from a book of antique botanical prints.

Charm School

THE SCHUMACHER GUIDE TO TRADITIONAL DECORATING FOR TODAY

EMMA BAZILIAN & STEPHANIE DIAZ

MONACELLI
SCHUMACHER

Barrie Benson used old-fashioned touches—gathered cabinet curtains, a plate-covered wall, a faux-bamboo chandelier—to create a cozy nook for family game nights.

Introduction 6

Chintz & Florals 10

Checks & Stripes 28

Toile 44

Matching 58

Skirts 72

Slipcovers 88

Bed Hangings 98

Window Treatments 108

Scallops 120

Wicker & Rattan 136

Treillage 150

Decorative Painting 164

Vintage & Antiques 176

Collections 192

Setting the Table 206

Making it Modern 216

Finishing Touches 234

Acknowledgements 250

I t's said that certain genetic traits tend to skip a generation. Red hair, for example, or color blindness. Or, based on personal experience, a strong affinity for floral chintz.

Born in the waning days of the 1980s to an interior decorator mother whose preferred palette (in furnishings as well as fashion) was black, white, and beige, I spent many of my childhood weekends at grandparents' houses, developing an interest in activities perhaps more suited to a retiree than a four-year-old girl—knitting and crocheting, watching early MGM musicals, bidding on antique dolls at auction. As the years went on, my parents watched, perplexed, as I insisted on outfitting my bedroom with Laura Ashley florals and toile; as a teenager, instead of sneaking out at night or piercing my nose, I took up needlepointing and amassed an enviable Lilly Pulitzer collection. "That looks like something your grandmother would wear," my mother would say as I tried on a frill-necked sweater; I took it as a compliment.

What proved most surprising was the fact that my fascination with this decidedly unfashionable aesthetic endured into adulthood—and that I wasn't alone. While the growing power of social media platforms like Instagram and Pinterest had overwhelmingly resulted in the embrace of a certain white-walled, minimalist-meets-midcentury aesthetic among its largely millennial audience, a ruffled rebellion was stirring on the fringes. Its members posted images of *decorated-with-a-capital-D* rooms by Sister Parish

and Mario Buatta, oohing and aahing over the kinds of rose-covered cushions and wicker chairs that their parents had long ago relegated to the basement; seemingly unaware that a well-stocked china cabinet had been declared extinct, they shared their latest hauls of vintage majolica and Staffordshire dogs.

In 2019, as an editor at *House Beautiful* magazine, I wrote about this growing interest around old-fashioned (or, some might say, outdated) decorating in an essay titled "The Rise of 'Grandmillennial' Style," then watched in shock as the portmanteau spread like wildfire across the internet, spawning hashtags and think pieces and Facebook groups. To these newly self-identified grandmillennials, it was a rallying cry; to others, it begged the question, why? To me, at least, the enduring appeal of traditionalism lies in its timelessness. In an age of disposability, of trends that come and go in the blink of an eye, there's a comfort in knowing that a certain Chippendale chair or hand-blocked chintz was as beguiling in the 1780s as it was in the 1980s as it still is today. Or that the needlepoint pillow stitched for a new baby will become a keepsake in the decades to come. Or that, despite what spartan fashions might prevail, sinking into an overstuffed, slipcovered sofa will never not feel divine.

In these pages, we've endeavored to both pay homage to the great designers of the past that helped define what we think of as traditional decor and to celebrate the modern-day talents bringing its familiar elements—skirted furniture, blowsy florals, treillage-covered walls—into the future. Whether the results are grand or humble, awash in bold color or more quietly elegant, what these rooms all share is a feeling of being inherently lived-in and, above all, well-loved. My own grandparents, I'd like to think, would very much approve.

- Emma Bazilian

OPPOSITE, CLOCKWISE FROM TOP LEFT: An unabashed fan of all things scalloped, Soane Britain founder Lulu Lytle paired a 19th-century chintz bedcover with a fabric of her own design in her daughter's bedroom. An 1830 folk-art document provided the inspiration for this hand-painted screen in a Maine living room designed by Lilse McKenna; in 2020s fashion, it hides a TV. CeCe Barfield Thompson created an ultra-feminine boudoir for the New York headquarters of fashion and decor brand Hill House Home. "Everybody knows I love chic-old-lady style," declared Miles Redd to *Architectural Digest* while discussing a floral-filled house he designed for a young Texas family.

Chintz
& Florals

For a textile with such buttoned-up associations, chintz has a surprisingly tumultuous history. Originating thousands of years ago in present-day India and Pakistan, printed chintz—its name derived from the Hindi *"chint,"* meaning speckled or spotted—began making its way to Europe in the 1500s. Its vivid colors and patterns proved so wildly irresistible that, by the late 17th century, more than a million pieces were being imported each year; countries like England and France, concerned that the popularity of Indian chintz was becoming a threat to its own domestic manufacturing, outlawed its import, going so far as to threaten smugglers with execution. Eventually, English mills figured out how to produce the glazed floral fabrics now synonymous with British country houses, fussy dresses, and 1980s excess. And with a new generation of designers rediscovering the undeniable charm of a motif so recently declared outré (if not exactly punishable by death these days), one might argue that chintz has become almost subversive once again.

FROM THE ARCHIVES
OPPOSITE, CLOCKWISE FROM TOP: Parish-Hadley decorated numerous residences for Betsey Cushing and John Hay "Jock" Whitney, including their Saratoga Springs, New York, house, where a grand painted bed provided a counterpoint to floral walls and curtains. A sofa in the home of Imogen Taylor, onetime principal at Sibyl Colefax & John Fowler, was re-covered in chintz by her father. The guest room of Hickory Hill, Robert F. Kennedy's home in Virginia, graced the cover of *House & Garden* in 1962.

A hand-painted botanical wallcovering transforms this Connecticut living room by Ashley Whittaker into a year-round garden. Simple shapes and geometric motifs—like a 19th-century spoon-back chair, bone-inlaid mirror, and trimmed Roman shades—temper the floral's sweetness.

"A lot of times, you see linear florals in dining rooms or foyers, but I thought it would be more interesting to do it in a living room," says Jenny Holladay of Summer Thornton Design, who used *Schumacher's Pyne Hollyhock wallpaper* in her Chicago townhouse. The curtains are in *Lange Glazed Linen*. OPPOSITE: Brimming with country charm, Rita Konig's former New York apartment features an explosion of fuchsias in the bedroom.

Miniature pastoral scenes within the wavy trellis border of *Marella fabric and wallpaper by Vogue Living for Schumacher* add whimsy to vintage pieces. OPPOSITE: *Schumacher's Hydrangea Drape*, designed in the 1930s by legendary set decorator Hobe Erwin, provides a backdrop for modern art and antique intaglios in John Bossard's Atlanta apartment. The chairs are in *Atwood Epingle*.

Even a hint of chintz can have a striking effect: In the pale-hued sunroom of a 1930s home by Ruthie Sommers, a pair of floral ottomans makes a romantic statement. Billy Baldwin—one of the house's original decorators—would surely approve.

21

An English garden's worth of rose-covered fabric
envelops a bedroom in a stately San Francisco home,
where Allison Caccoma curated a mix of period antiques,
reproductions and finds from the client's travels.

23

Markham Roberts makes a strong case for floral-on-floral; a thread of blue unifies the trio of patterns. OPPOSITE: Similarly, Vanrenen GW Designs proves that a jumble of stripes, blooms and block prints makes for a particularly cozy retreat.

Bowood House in Wiltshire, England serves as the namesake for this classic Colefax & Fowler pattern; its current owner, Fiona Lansdowne, swathed nearly every surface of one guest room in a rosy colorway.

Checks
& Stripes

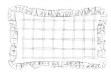

Few motifs are quite as chameleon-like as the humble stripe. Deployed in wide swaths, à la Dorothy Draper, a stripe can read dramatic and strong; a slim ticking stripe, a favorite of Sister Parish's, exudes quaint country charm. Use a vertical stripe to give the illusion of height, or a horizontal one to make a space feel more intimate; run it on the bias along cushions or trim to add a bit of unpredictability. Its cousin, the check, is an equally adaptable player, able to manifest as an airy windowpane, a graphic checkerboard, or a stately tartan plaid with just a slight shift of its intersecting lines. While stripes and checks are both natural companions for other patterns, they're more than capable of being the stars of their own show: Tent a room in stripes to create a Mongiardino-esque escape, or channel Gloria Vanderbilt and go for broke (metaphorically) with ginghams of every scale and size. Extra points for dressing to match.

Georgian goes glam in a tented room in London boutique hotel Henry's House, once home to Jane Austen's brother. OPPOSITE: Wide stripes and oversize checks add an unexpected jolt of English whimsy to the natural textures of a Portuguese villa designed by David Hicks.

A checkerboard-patterned chair feels fresh against a chinoiserie mural in a living room by Rosanna Bossom. OPPOSITE, CLOCKWISE FROM TOP LEFT: A checked roman shade lends country elegance to a cozy bath by Salvesen Graham. A celadon claw-foot tub calls for an equally charming shower curtain in *Pauline Check Casement by Vogue Living for Schumacher;* the towel is in *Schumacher's Jean Stripe.* A pink-and-green bedroom by Meredith Ellis provides a sweet retreat for twin girls. Natasha Haberman paired an antique wooden chair with curtain in *Schumacher's Camden Check* for a study in opposites.

34

A checked tablecloth and a bevy of natural materials sets a
laid-back tone in a dining nook by Billy Cotton. OPPOSITE: A
picnic-ready gingham ceiling and folk-art-inspired painted floor
make this kitchen by Anthony Baratta a joyous ode to Americana.

A crisp blue-striped tablecloth and antique Gustavian dining chairs add Swedish flavor to textile designer Louise Townsend's English cottage.

Mark D. Sikes gives gingham and wicker a globe-trotting update in his Los Angeles dining room. OPPOSITE: For a show house room, Sikes channeled design icons Renzo Mongiardino and Marella Agnelli with maximalist results; the walls are covered in *Elton Check* fabric by Schumacher.

A chunky striped lampshade contrasts with the swirls of a Murano glass base in a living room by Sarah Brown. OPPOSITE: Rachel Chudley wrapped a London nursery in a riot of stripes to highlight the angles of the attic room.

Toile

Like chintz, the word "toile" has come to encompass much more than its earliest definition as a type of woven cloth. For that, we can thank the German-born Christophe-Philipe Oberkampf, who in 1760 opened a factory in Jouy-en-Josas, near Versailles, that began printing the pastoral *toiles de Jouy* we know and love today. The images depicted in toiles have continued to evolve with changing trends—architectural vistas grew popular as wealthy Europeans embarked on the *grand tour*, patriotic scenes celebrated the American and French revolutions, more modern interpretations have featured everything from Harlem playgrounds to headphone-wearing cherubs—but the appeal of a lightly sketched monochrome design printed on solid (often white) ground hasn't diminished. Used as an all-over motif or just an accent, a good toile never goes out of style.

FROM THE ARCHIVES
OPPOSITE, CLOCKWISE FROM TOP LEFT: "Toile makes such a strong visual statement you don't need other patterns," decorator Mary Meehan told *House Beautiful* in 1987. Madeleine Castaing framed toile-covered wall panels with elegant gray trim. Imogen Taylor, the principal decorator at Colefax & Fowler from the 70s through the 90s, decked out a spare bedroom in a rose and cream print.

A French toile goes full Americana in the red, white and blue bedroom of John Knott and John Fondas's Maine vacation house. OPPOSITE: *Schumacher's Marine Toile fabric* was paper-backed for the walls of a nautically infused Cape Cod summer home. FOLLOWING PAGES, FROM LEFT: An acid green ground adds youthful energy to the toile wallpaper in design editor Tori Mellott's former Brooklyn kitchen. Sheila Bridges's Harlem Toile, reconceived with vignettes of the historic Manhattan neighborhood, is a modern-day classic. Designer Katy Barker pairs toiles in rich chocolate brown and vibrant tangerine-and-fuchsia for an exuberant bedroom.

Textile historian Jill Lasersohn's infatuation with toiles is evident in her New York apartment, where designer Marshall Watson used her *Les Losanges wallpaper for Schumacher* in the entryway. OPPOSITE: Lasersohn's *Chariot of Dawn wallpaper* expands a classical motif to a mural-sized scale. FOLLOWING PAGES, FROM LEFT: Tory Burch and decorator Daniel Romualdez channel English manor house living in the fashion mogul's Hamptons home. A patchwork quilt adds humble charm to a grand canopied bed and toile de Jouy wallcovering in a home by Thierry Zali. Melissa Ervin illustrates the staying power of a traditional toile-on-toile room.

In a New Orleans bedroom, Brockschmidt & Coleman capture
the steamy-yet-refined mood of the French Quarter with a
combination of toile, ticking stripes and millwork in juicy mango.

Matching

Like so many of the decorating trends that reached fever pitch in the 1980s, dressing a room in a single print or pattern has become something of a decorating *don't* in the present day. But take it from Billy Baldwin and Renzo Mongiardino: A series of co-ordinating elements—wallpaper, curtains and upholstery, yes, but also accessories like lamp shades and luggage racks, and perhaps even a few case goods—can have a marvelously mesmerizing effect, wrapping a space's inhabitants in a warm embrace. (Designers will tell you that this strategy can be especially successful in a small room, which already lends itself to a jewel-box-like atmosphere.) So go ahead and match walls to window treatments and bedding to bergères without reserve—if it was good enough for Henri Samuel, who are we to argue?

FROM THE ARCHIVES

OPPOSITE, CLOCKWISE FROM TOP LEFT: Lily-of-the-valley printed glazed chintz was a favorite of Frances Elkins, who used it in the homes of clients including Marshall and Evelyn Field in the 1930s. Dubbed "one of the high-water marks of 20th-century decoration" by *The New York Times*, the "Salon Bleu" that Henri Samuel created for Louise de Vilmorin was awash in batik-style cotton. Another of Elkins's rooms for the Fields featured a trailing floral print on walls, windows, and even a dressing table. Thomas Britt created a tented bath with bold red-and-white stripes.

A petite folding screen seems to practically disappear against matching wallpaper in a bathroom designed by Gabby Deeming for *House & Garden* UK; the powder-blue tub breaks up the mass of flowers. OPPOSITE: When going all out with a single print, a classic pattern—like this small-scale blue-and-white floral used by Cathy Kincaid—is always a smart choice.

From valances to walls (and even the luggage rack), nearly every surface of this bedroom in the home of Stubbs & Wootton founder Percy Steinhart is swathed in Colefax & Fowler's Bowood, while accents appear in varying shades of green—not all matching, but harmonious nonetheless.

It might seem counterintuitive, but wall-to-wall pattern and a four-poster bed help make a small bedroom feel cozy, not claustrophobic; here, Miles Redd used his *Dogwood Leaf* fabric for Schumacher. OPPOSITE: A festive canopy takes pride of place in a pattern-filled room by Katie Ridder.

A subtle strip of blue tape below the crown molding and along curtain edges in Caroline Gidiere's guest bedroom adds structure to the large expanses of botanical pattern.

Mikaela Irwin carefully lined up the trailing vines of the wallcovering and upholstered headboard for a seamless effect. OPPOSITE: For a creative take on pattern-on-pattern, Tom Scheerer had a bedroom dresser custom-painted to match the floral wallpaper.

Skirts

A well-placed skirt can hide a multitude of sins. That teetering pile of clutter under a hall table? Gone. A few friendly dust bunnies hiding beneath the bed? Poof. Cleaning supplies crowded around the bathroom sink? No one will be the wiser. Of course, a skirt applied for purely aesthetic reasons is just as compelling: Whether loosely gathered, crisply pleated, or lavishly billowing, it provides a charming respite from a sea of table legs and cabinet fronts—not to mention the opportunity to deploy more fabric. (May we suggest a vintage chintz?) The ditsy cousin of the skirt, the ruffle is an unabashed declaration of whimsy, a triumph of form over function. Add one (or two) to a pillow or lampshade for a daily reminder that pretty for pretty's sake is *always* a good idea.

A skirted dressing table makes even the most harried morning routine feel delightfully indulgent. Swing-out arms on a striped vanity by Barrie Benson open to reveal hidden storage space. OPPOSITE: Swathed in frills of frothy pink silk, the kidney-shaped dressing table in Alice Naylor-Leyland's bedroom (designed by Flora Soames) is the epitome of feminine glamour.

Toile de la Prairie by Jill Lasersohn for Schumacher conceals cocktail-hour accoutrements in the designer's Hamptons home. OPPOSITE: *Tucked into the corner of Lilse McKenna's former Brooklyn kitchen, a skirted table and shelves make for a well-dressed bar.*

A lush green table cloth with tone-on-tone trim and plenty of blue-and-white porcelain create classic grandeur in a Greenwich, Connecticut, home designed by Sarah Bartholomew. PRECEDING PAGES, FROM LEFT: A trio of trims gussies up a solid skirted table in a Connecticut living room by Ashley Whittaker. Rebecca de Ravenel used a block-printed cloth to casually drape her bedside table. Floor-sweeping tassels make a pale blue tablecloth feel suitably dressy in Caroline Gidiere's formal dining room; she used *Chinoiserie Vine fabric by Mark D. Sikes for Schumacher* on the chair seats.

Whether short and sweet or falling gracefully to the floor, a chair skirt never fails to delight. Smart pleats make this one by Salvesen Graham more streamlined. OPPOSITE, CLOCKWISE FROM TOP LEFT: Contrast welting in a deep aubergine, pulled from the blooms of *Schumacher's Salisbury Chintz*, outlines a chair in Jenny Holladay's living room. A vanity stool in ballerina pink adds softness to a young girl's bath; the wallpaper is *Harbury Trellis by Schumacher*. A subtle stripe of blue tape runs along the bottom of a chair in Ashley Whittaker's house. Rita Konig takes the fuss out of frill with easygoing linen. FOLLOWING PAGES, FROM LEFT: Matilda Goad used clip-on curtain rings to hang a clutter-concealing chintz panel in her pantry. A zigzag cabinet frame and a mix of printed textiles feel wonderfully energetic in a kitchen vignette styled by Gabby Deeming and Ruth Sleightholme. Wrap a pedestal sink in a favorite fabric for instant storage in a pint-size powder room; the skirt is in *Pauline Check casement* and the wallpaper is *Adele*, both by *Vogue Living for Schumacher*.

Slipcovers

As is the case with so many staples of traditional decorating, the slipcover was born out of practicality. Used on sofas and chairs in the warmer months, slipcovers protected upholstery from any dust and pollen wafting through open windows—and from inhabitants' sweaty bodies. With the advent of air conditioning, those needs largely dissipated, but slipcovers remained a favorite designer trick nonetheless. Billy Baldwin brought a new sense of ease to high-society interiors by cloaking his favorite slipper chairs in cotton; the great English decorators covered well-worn sofas with ruffled chintz ones. Even now, slipcovers are an indispensable addition to any home with children, pets, or red-wine drinkers. Keep the look sleek with tailored covers, or embrace a cottage ambiance with loose, rumpled linen. Either way, your furniture will thank you.

A quintessentially English floral covers a
quintessentially English roll-arm sofa, styled by Gabby
Deeming. OPPOSITE: A skirted sofa veers playfully
bohemian in a joyously colorful room by Anna Spiro.

Anne Wagoner slipcovered a high-backed chair in a wavy fern print, creating a quiet moment in a colorful, chintz-filled bedroom. OPPOSITE: Dressmaker details on a set of chairs in a dining room by Sarah Bartholomew are buttoned up in all the right ways.

In her Birmingham, Alabama, home,
Caroline Gidiere uses ruffled slipcovers
in Colefax & Fowler's Bowood to add an
air of easy elegance to formal furnishings.

Bed Hangings

Mastering the vocabulary of canopy beds—originally designed to keep out drafts on cold winter nights and provide privacy in shared quarters—can feel a bit like enrolling in a French course: There's the *lit à colonnes*, or classic four-poster canopy bed; *the lit à couronne*, whose curtains hang from a "crown" suspended above the head of the bed; the *lit à la polonaise*, which features small central canopy supported by four curved posts; the *lit à la turque*, essentially a canopied daybed; and the *lit à duchesse*, or tester bed. If it all gets a bit confusing, fear not: All you really need to worry about is whether to use your favorite floral print, a sumptuous silk taffeta, or an airy cotton gauze.

FROM THE ARCHIVES
OPPOSITE, CLOCKWISE FROM TOP LEFT: Pauline Boardman left no curtain untrimmed in this sumptuous bedroom, adding bows, tassels and pleats to a *lit à la polonaise*. Dubbed "the bedroom that shook the world" by *Architectural Digest*, Mario Buatta's 1984 Kips Bay Show House room—which featured a frothy white canopy bed as its centerpiece—earned him the nickname "The Prince of Chintz." Clean tailoring and crisp checks defined a pair of half-tester beds designed by John Scoville.

A more laid-back take on a *lit à la polonaise* feels right for a house in the tropics; Amanda Lindroth draped the bed in a sheer block print. OPPOSITE: Hand-embroidered flowers and pom-pom trim embellish a *lit à couronne* in a fanciful-yet-sophisticated London bedroom by Alidad.

Matilda Goad used panels of simple white linen to soften a vintage four-poster bed in her London bedroom. OPPOSITE: A set of curtains adds an extra layer of privacy to a tucked-away bunk in the dressing room of Philip Mitchell's Nova Scotia summer cottage.

Inspired by a Syrie Maugham design, a half-tester canopy provides visual respite from the bold floral fabric lining the walls of a bedroom by Ashley Whittaker. OPPOSITE: Veere Grenney draped a canopy bed in a blue-and-white floral print for a London client; the decorative edging evokes a Medieval tent.

Window Treatments

There is, supposedly, a case to be made for bare windows. But for a certain type of decorator, allowing a window to go undressed is akin to stepping out on Fifth Avenue stark naked. Certainly a set of simple pinch-pleated curtains or relaxed romans can be a good place to start, but why not up the ante with something a bit more baroque, like a billowing balloon shade, festoon blind or theatrical swag? An upholstered pelmet can add a sense of architecture to a blank-box room; panels of lace or eyelet are unexpectedly fresh when employed with a light touch. Hang curtains from the very top of the room for an illusion of added height and let them puddle dramatically on the floor. And don't forget the trimmings: A tasseled tieback, contrasting tape or bouncy ball fringe can be exactly what a room needs for that bit of extra oomph.

Brittany Bromley designed these dramatic window treatments using unlined *Botticelli Silk Taffeta by Schumacher;* pale pink *Etienne Silk Greek Key tape by Schumacher* runs along the leading edge of the curtain panels as a subtle finishing touch. The painted floor is an homage to the late Bunny Mellon's Billy Baldwin–designed house in Antigua.

Temper a busy wallpaper with solid (but luxe) relaxed roman shades, like Allison Caccoma did in a client's sunny San Francisco bedroom. PRECEDING PAGES, FROM LEFT: Barrie Benson chose simple cotton striped curtains to break up the formality of a Greenwich, Connecticut, study; the same fabric, on the bias, adds contrast to edges. Dramatic swagged curtains are lightened with playful touches, like pom-pom trim and Granny Smith apple green lining, in a room by Matthew Bees. Ruthie Sommers trimmed curtains with a perky silk flounce: the sofa is in *Gainsborough Velvet by Schumacher.*

Richly hued curtains, with vintage trim on the valance,
suit the historic flavor of Markham Roberts's Hudson Valley,
New York, home without competing with the patterned walls.

Scallops

Perhaps it's no surprise that four of the five definitions for "scal-lop" in Webster's dictionary describe something consumable: Whenever an object is adorned with the *fifth* definition—"one of a continuous series of circle segments or angular projections forming a border"—we just want to eat it right up. A scalloped edge elevates the everyday, adding a playful bit of fun to just about any object, be it a simple console table, a bathroom sink, a window shade, or the perimeter of a bedsheet. (There's even a case to be made for scalloped pantry shelves in the following pages.) It can be attention-grabbing or subtle, each section dramatically rounded or softly undulating. However you slice it (quite literally), a scalloped detail will always enchant.

FROM THE ARCHIVES
OPPOSITE, CLOCKWISE FROM TOP: A wavy-edged bedspread mirrored the silhouette of the canopy above in a bedroom by William Haines. With its tassels and stripes, a bold scalloped awning at the home of Ruth Rathell Tippett was pure 1960s Hollywood glamour. A 19th-century painted table displayed potted plants in the home of Stanley Falconer, a decorator at Sibyl Colefax & John Fowler.

A scalloped rattan chaise and plenty of flamingo pink make for an updated take on Palm Beach decorating in a showhouse room by Suzanne Kasler. OPPOSITE: Petal-like scallops, fern-green millwork and plenty of natural materials add garden charm to designer Ariel Okin's mudroom. The bench seat is in *Smithton Weave* by *Schumacher.* FOLLOWING PAGES, FROM LEFT: A scalloped edge is a sweet addition to an empire shade in a room by Rita Konig; the curtains are in *Pomegranate Print by Schumacher.* In her London flat, Konig used a scalloped edge to dress up a simple linen slipcover. A shell-shaped Soane Britain chair adds an eclectic touch in a floral-filled space by Henry & Co.; the *Petal Abaca* rug is from *Patterson Flynn.*

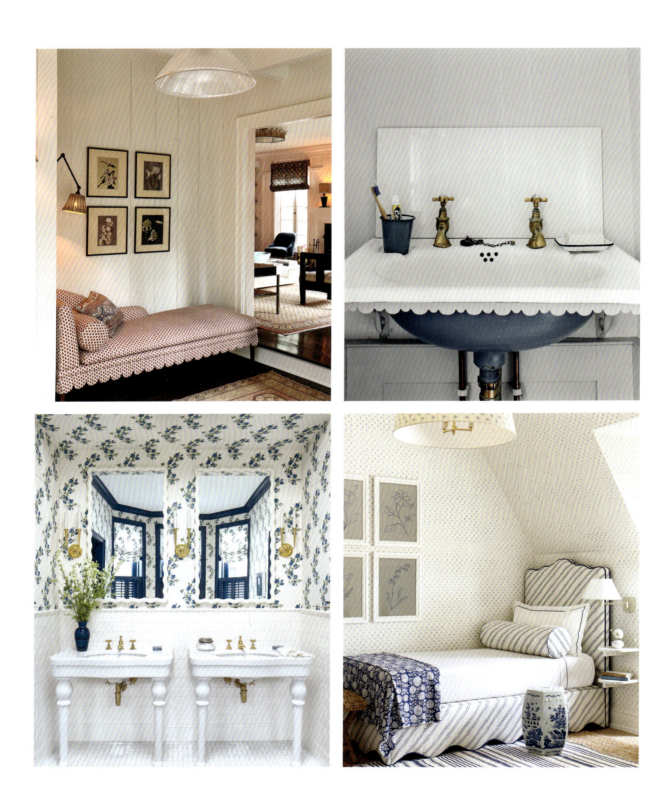

CLOCKWISE FROM TOP LEFT: A tucked-in daybed in a Nickey Kehoe-designed Los Angeles home calls for curling up with a book. Patrick Williams, whose building firm Berdoulat specializes in period restorations, found this vintage basin on eBay. A bias stripe highlights the wavy lines of a bed by Sarah Bartholomew. "English quirkiness" was the inspiration behind a Summer Thornton–designed bathroom. OPPOSITE: Scallops feel more clean than cutesy in the hands of Veere Grenney, who used *Schumacher's Lismore Linen Plain* for the window treatments.

Celerie Kemble dressed up a tailored, tufted sofa with a whimsically wavy back for a sitting room at the Mayflower Inn in Connecticut; the windowpane pillows are in *Marietta by Schumacher*.

Custom-designed beds with undulating canopies, upholstered in a small-scale printed fabric, feel fresh flanking an 18th-century chinoiserie commode in this bedroom designed by Olasky & Sinsteden.

Barrie Benson exaggerated the scale of the scalloped edges on a pair of curtains for a more modern take on the motif. OPPOSITE: Scalloped millwork and sunshine-yellow paint take a pantry by Salvesen Graham from utilitarian to uplifting.

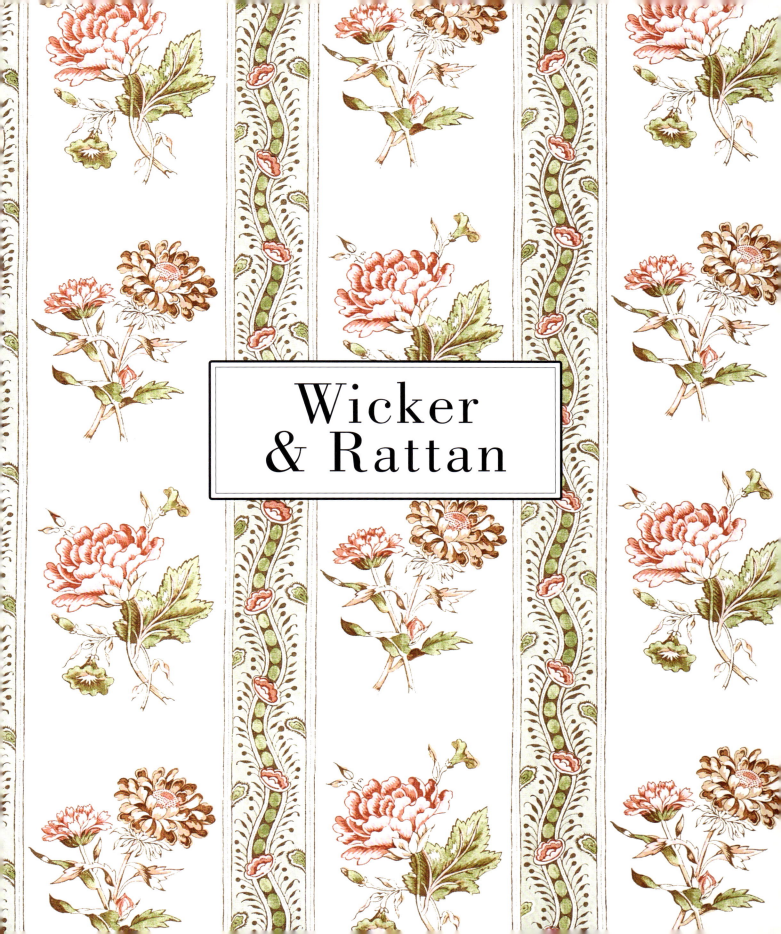

Wicker
& Rattan

First things first: Wicker and rattan are not the same thing. *Rattan* is a type of climbing palm comprising some 600 species, which grow primarily in the rainforests of Southeast Asia. *Wicker* is a 5,000-year-old weaving method—often but not always using rattan—used to make light-but-sturdy baskets, furniture and even the occasional piece of armor. (Soldiers in ancient Persia were said to have used wicker shields—how chic!) Nowadays, wickerwork is likelier to be found on the porch than the battlefield, but that doesn't mean it should be relegated solely to the outdoors. (Most rattan isn't even waterproof, anyway.) Take a cue from Sister Parish and fill a room with painted wicker furniture for an instant dose of old-school charm, or keep it more modern with the types of clean-lined, natural rattan pieces famously favored by Hubert de Givenchy. It's the next best thing to being on holiday year-round.

FROM THE ARCHIVES

OPPOSITE, FROM TOP: The conservatory of Countess Cristiana Brandolini d'Adda's estate in Veneto, Italy—Renzo Mongiardino's first project—was decorated with white-painted rattan. Elsewhere in Italy, director Franco Zeffirelli filled the terrace of his Amalfi Coast villa, Tre Ville, with wicker furniture.

In her colorful London flat, Soane Britain founder Lulu Lytle painted an Eastern-inspired rattan table in a rich shade of jade green. OPPOSITE: Repurposed from a client's own childhood bedroom, a pair of white wicker beds was given new life in a Florida guest room by Tom Scheerer.

A profusion of wicker furniture, floral prints and towering plants blurs the divide between Mark D. Sikes's California living room and the garden right outside the arched French doors.

145

On the porch of Markham Roberts and James Sansum's 1870s home in the Pacific Northwest, painted wicker furniture feels old-fashioned but not precious. OPPOSITE, CLOCKWISE FROM TOP LEFT: A rattan bar cart brings the party outdoors at Whitney McGregor's South Carolina house; a daybed in *Albert Performance fabric by Schumacher* can withstand spills. White rattan sets a bright mood at an Adirondack home designed by G.P. Schafer Architect. Another view of Markham Roberts's porch. G.P. Schafer restored and outfitted the 19th-century William C. Gatewood House in Charleston, South Carolina, with historically appropriate painted wicker.

Black-painted wicker furniture and muntins add subtle contrast to tailored upholstery and a wordly array of fabrics in a sunroom designed by Barrie Benson.

Treillage

In February, 1907, the New York Times regaled readers with a dispatch from the soon-to-open Colony Club, which boasted interiors by up-and-coming society decorator Elsie de Wolfe. "One of the most interesting rooms," declared the newspaper, "is the tea room...The walls are trellised in green, and in the centre of the room a fountain plays. The effect is most restful and pleasing, and no doubt it will prove one of the most attractive and popular places within the house." While de Wolfe wasn't the first to bring treillage indoors—it had been a popular decorating trick in 18th-century French chateaux—the stir created by her tearoom helped catapult her to design stardom (and spawned a slew of imitators). More than a century later, it's still easy to see why: Whether applied in the form of actual woodwork or mimicked via wallpaper or brushstroke, treillage has the power to transform any room into a garden of earthly delights.

Paloma Contreras put her own updated spin on old-school Floridian decorating for the Kips Bay Palm Beach showhouse. Applied to walls and ceiling in a straight grid, latticework feels graphic and fresh; valances mimic the motif. The chairs are in *Dogwood Leaf by Miles Redd*, pillows are in *Wellfleet Ticking Stripe* and curtains are *Lange Glazed Linen by Schumacher*.

Celerie Kemble elevated standard lattice with millwork frames at Connecticut's Mayflower Inn; papier-mâché bows and botanicals make it a sweet confection. OPPOSITE: In a dressing room by Henri Garelli, mirror set behind delicate trelliswork casts a sparkling glow.

FROM TOP: Summer Thornton created a "Victorian fantasy full of ferns, flowers, and latticework" in her family's Chicago sunroom, painting the walls boxwood green to add contrast to the white trellis. Asia Baker Stokes puts a more modern spin on trellis and wicker in a historic house in Cold Spring Harbor, New York. OPPOSITE: *Schumacher's Bermuda Check, Garden Gate Chintz* and plenty of treillage turn a young girl's bedroom by The Fox Group into an enchanted garden.

A trellised indoor pool room by Paul Garzotto exudes 1930s glamour. OPPOSITE: A shower enclosure inspired by the gazebo at Old Westbury Gardens on Long Island makes for a fanciful centerpiece in a bathroom designed by Anthony Baratta.

161

Bunny Williams used hand-painted wallpaper to create the illusion of a treillage-covered room in a Georgian-style Virginia home.

Decorative Painting

From Ancient Greece to the palaces of Renaissance Italy, paint has long been used to create visual trickery in interiors. It can add fanciful architecture to a room that has none, cover a bare wall in charming treillage, turn a plain wood floor into a colorfully tiled one, or create sweeping pastoral vistas where no window exists. Although stenciling was once used as an inexpensive substitute for fine wallcovering, the technique is regaining regard among designers who appreciate its pefectly imperfect feel. In fact, sometimes a trompe-l'oeil take on lavish materials like plasterwork or precious stone can feel even more extravagant than the real thing.

FROM THE ARCHIVES
OPPOSITE, CLOCKWISE FROM TOP LEFT: Artist Lyn LeGrice used stencils to create a whimsical nursery in her 18th-century home in Cornwall, England. A self-proclaimed fanatic for painted floors, onetime Parish-Hadley decorator Libby Cameron designed this faux-bois motif for a client's farmhouse. In Bunny Mellon's garden room at Oak Spring, her country estate in Virginia, painter Fernand Renard created a trompe-l'oeil masterpiece. Born to a wealthy New England family in 1792, artist and inventor Rufus Porter's primitive murals are a touchstone of early Americana.

A scenic mural is a timeless choice. Here, Meredith Ellis decorated the walls of a Dallas showhouse bath to transport visitors to coastal New England. OPPOSITE: Inspired by the ornate plasterwork at Claydon House in England, artist Aldous Bertram painted trompe-l'oeil friezes on the walls of Amanda Lindroth's "blank box" Palm Beach living room. FOLLOWING PAGES: Painted checkerboard floors feel just right in the Hamptons home of Kate Rheinstein Brodsky (left) and a bathroom by British design firm Salvesen Graham (right). A lemon-yellow floor by Miles Redd for Erika Bearman (center) casts a sunny glow no matter the weather.

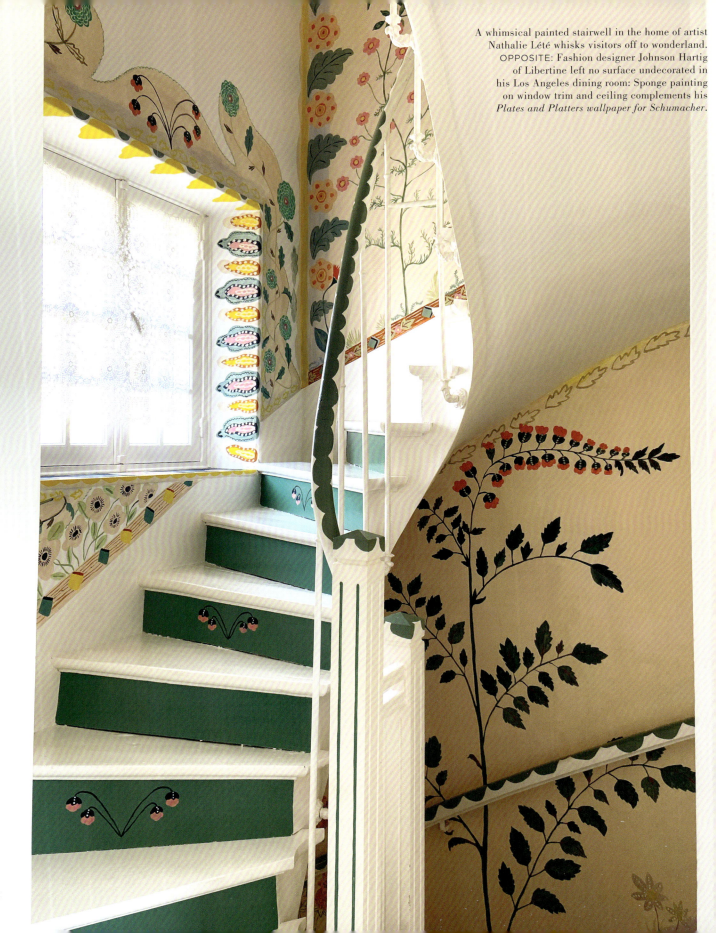

A whimsical painted stairwell in the home of artist Nathalie Lété whisks visitors off to wonderland. OPPOSITE: Fashion designer Johnson Hartig of Libertine left no surface undecorated in his Los Angeles dining room: Sponge painting on window trim and ceiling complements his *Plates and Platters* wallpaper for Schumacher.

In a charming pink-and-green bedroom, Annie Sloan used her signature chalk paint on furniture and walls to create simple scallops and stripes. OPPOSITE: Gabby Deeming embellished a vintage armoire with botanical motifs using Sloan's paint.

Vintage
& Antiques

Spend any length of time scrolling through furniture listings on Craigslist and you'll quickly notice a recurring theme: brown furniture. Once a hallmark of any well-furnished home, suites of heavy mahogany and walnut have gone the way of rotary phones and VHS players; those who do pick up such pieces at estate and yard sales will often give them a coat of paint before putting them to use. But before you take a paintbrush to granny's English breakfront or drop off those Federal-style chairs at a consignment shop, flip through the following pages for proof that even the dustiest old antique has potential when used in the right setting. While furnishing your bedroom with a full matching set might feel a little too dated, that Chippendale chest could add a sense of gravitas you never knew you needed.

While Michael Devine and Thomas Burak's house in Virginia was built in the 1950s, it has a distinctly Colonial-era sensibility. "White walls with a strong trim feels very 18th-century," says Devine, who had the electric chandelier converted to candlelight. OPPOSITE: The clear celadon blue of *Schumacher's Gainsborough Velvet* on a chair in Markham Roberts's Hudson Valley home lifts moody floral walls and a stately 19th-century American chest of drawers.

In Colonial Williamsburg's Palmer House, built in 1750, Designer in Residence Anthony Baratta used black-painted Windsor chairs to temper the bright—but historically accurate—paint colors, inspired by the Williamsburg Fife and Drum Corps.

Designer Cameron Kimber designed his sitting room around a small Bessarabian rug; because it was far too small for the space, he layered it on top of simple straw matting. Antique paintings add gravitas to the bright white walls. PRECEDING PAGES, FROM LEFT: From formal settings to laid-back rooms, even "serious" antiques can be surprisingly versatile. Abstract art flanks a stately chest in Matthew Bees's Charleston bedroom. Ashley Whittaker makes dark wood feel at home with colorful block prints and bright white scallops. A black chinoiserie highboy grounds a palette of blues and whites in Sarah Bartholomew's Nashville home.

CLOCKWISE FROM TOP LEFT: Pink adds perk to a dark wood bedside table and brown fabric-covered walls *(Schumacher's Pomegranate Print)* in a bedroom by Rita Konig. Charlotte Barnes transformed an old dresser into a new vanity for her powder room. *Avebury Floral Vine by Schumacher* was the starting point for a room filled with vintage finds by Pencil & Paper Co.; they also used *Schumacher's Soho Diamond Wallpaper, Astara Paisley fabric* (on stools) and *Sabine Braid* (on lampshade). "I think every room needs a bit of brown furniture to make it feel collected and authentic," says designer Jenny Holladay, who paired her great-grandmother's George III end tables with custom lampshades in a breezy blue-and-white print; the headboard is in *Brigitte Stripe by Schumacher*. OPPOSITE: Markham Roberts converted a 19th-century washstand into a working sink in his Hudson Valley house.

Celerie Kemble mixed high and low in the Mayflower Inn, hanging museum-quality pieces alongside "silly and pretty and bright" eBay finds. "It's about having a critical mass of non-matching pieces so everything feels in balance," she says.

Ser

191

Collections

Jackie Kennedy scoured Cape Cod in search of vintage Sandwich glass. C.Z. Guest and Bunny Mellon filled their homes with majolica and lettuceware. Princess Diana added a new Herend figurine to her collection each Christmas. Mario Buatta spent his career amassing treasure troves of, well, just about everything. (Among them: 19th-century dog paintings, needlepoint pillows, Delft china, and fruit-shaped enamel boxes.) A beloved collection, passed down through generations or just recently begun, has the power to imbue a room with its owner's singular personality, telling a story or begging for one to be told. The key: Display collections loudly and proudly, whether they're priceless antiques or price-*less* knick knacks. Let a great-aunt's plates fill an entire dining room wall, hang botanical prints froom floor to ceiling, and cover entire shelves with Limoges boxes, dust be damned. And remember—there's always room for just one more. Because it's not hoarding, it's *collecting*.

FROM THE ARCHIVES
OPPOSITE, CLOCKWISE FROM TOP LEFT: A collection of Fabergé boxes in Diane von Furstenburg's New York apartment, photographed in the 1970s. Decorator Ann LeConey "has become somewhat obsessed" with Staffordshire, wrote *House Beautiful* in 1986; "her figurines overflow kitchen shelves and living room tables." Celebrated art collector Jayne Wrightsman displayed Meissen porcelain birds in her Henri Samuel–designed Palm Beach living room. Eighteenth-century majolica filled a hallway at Bunny Mellon's Oak Spring estate.

Libertine's Johnson Hartig describes his Los Angeles home, overflowing with pattern and color, as "grandmotherly." Gathered over 25 years, Hartig's collection of baskets inspired the house's name, "Basket Case." OPPOSITE: In the living room, Hartig curated an assortment of portraits from a variety of far-flung places and eras. The chair is covered in *Jokhang Tiger Velvet by Johnson Hartig/ Libertine for Schumacher;* the pillow on the far right is in *Nancy fabric by Schumacher.*

Striking teal walls mimic the hues found in a collection of majolica plates in the home of Frank de Biasi and Gene Meyer. PRECEDING PAGES, FROM LEFT: Classic blue-and-white porcelain matches the bedding in Les Indiennes founder Mary Mulcahy's guest room. Electric yellow walls are a refreshing backdrop to traditional blue-and-white china in Johnson Hartig's former Los Angeles home. Once relegated to the china cabinet, a set of Limoges fish plates handed down to Philip Mitchell by his mother and grandmother form a tidy grid on the walls of his butler's pantry and stairwell.

CLOCKWISE FROM TOP LEFT: "My bookshelves change every day with additions and subtractions of objects and books," says artist Mary Maguire, who added an extra dimension by hanging her shell-framed ship painting from the millwork. John Derian découpage trays create a wallpaper-like effect in a bathroom designed by Lilse McKenna. Varying shapes make this selection of avian prints in Sarah Bartholomew's Nashville home feel less static. OPPOSITE: With the help of stylist and friend Emma Burns, garden designer Butter Wakefield filled her London kitchen with a fitting mix of flora and fauna. PRECEDING PAGES, FROM LEFT: A colorful mix of new and old glassware adds sparkle to a cupboard in Charlotte Barnes's dining room. Ashley Whittaker painted the interior of a bleached-mahogany cabinet a striking shade of blue to compliment a client's Dodie Thayer lettuceware. *Marella wallpaper by Vogue Living for Schumacher* makes a fitting backdrop for blue-and-white china and creamware.

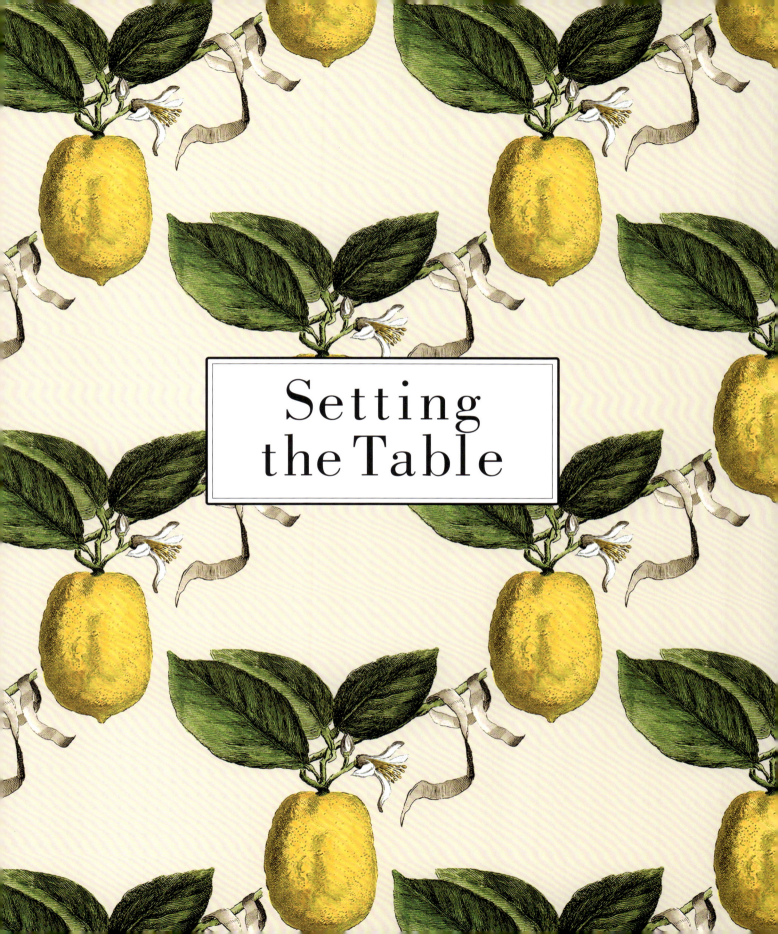

Setting
the Table

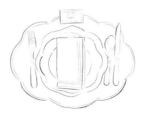

In the modern day, breaking out the "good china" often requires an occasion of great importance, like Thanksgiving dinner or a visiting head of state. And that, of course, is if said "good china" even exists; in an age of dishwashers, the thought of hand-wash-only plates can be enough to make any host or hostess shudder. But a new generation is embracing the pleasure of properly (or even not-so-properly) laying a table, mixing and matching pretty printed linens, sparkling glassware, flower-filled vases, and flickering candles, making a weekend dinner party with friends feel as festive as a grand soirée. We might not "dress for dinner" any more, but our tables certainly can.

Colored glassware adds punch to an old-fashioned floral chintz tablecloth in Land of Belle founder Annabelle Moehlmann's Upper East Side studio. OPPOSITE: *Schumacher's Garden Gate wallpaper* is the backdrop for another of Moehlmann's sweet-yet-sophisticated table settings.

Romantic blooms and floral fabrics (the chairs are upholstered in *Marella* and the napkins are *Bunny*, both by *Vogue Living for Schumacher*) add charm to a rustic farmhouse table. OPPOSITE: Thomas O'Brien repurposed an antique suzani as a tablecloth for an alfresco meal in the garden of his seaside home; blue-and-white faience dishes are the same pattern that Claude Monet used at Giverny.

213

The bluestone patio of Caroline Gidiere's Birmingham, Alabama home is an ideal setting for a weekend brunch. OPPOSITE: In Tory Burch's Antigua vacation home, once owned by Bunny Mellon, Dodie Thayer lettuceware gets a fresh update in an all-white palette.

Making it
Modern

As much as we might swoon over a space swathed in chintz or window treatments that require a circus tent's worth of fabric, being *overly* wedded to old-fashioned tropes can push a room perilously close to Miss Havisham territory. (Not that she didn't seem marvelously chic in her own mournful way.) What defines so many of the great design talents of the past and present is their ability to curate an anachronistic mix of old and new that feels natural and effortless—and a little bit surprising. In the mid-20th century, Henri Samuel ushered in a new era of French decorating by pairing modern pieces with antiques; today, the most exciting newcomers are combining Victorian motifs with midcentury shapes and hanging contemporary art above ruffle-skirted sofas. It's that deft mix of past and present that is destined to bring traditional decorating into the future.

FROM THE ARCHIVES
OPPOSITE, CLOCKWISE FROM TOP: Antique beds jumped from the past when paired with giant strawberry-print fabric and Lucite stools in this Parish-Hadley—designed bedroom. Diminutive bows added an unexpected sweet accent to this pared-down room in John Stefanidis's own London home. Billy Baldwin turned traditional slipcovers into a mod moment by using denim.

A custom-designed banquette, with cushions covered in hard-wearing denim, makes Matilda Goad's breakfast nook an ideal spot for family meals. The relaxed roman shades in an airy floral are a fresh note. FOLLOWING PAGES, FROM LEFT: An antique wicker dining set—complete with heart-shaped folding chairs—plus a Japanese paper lantern make Rebecca de Ravenel's Los Angeles dining area feel of-the-moment. An espalier-patterned wallpaper subtly reflects the linear nature of the New York City skyline, says Lilse McKenna. "We used Indian textiles and modern elements to keep it from feeling too preppy or traditional," Barrie Benson notes of this sunny kitchen nook.

221

Modern art and a midcentury Saarinen table are
unexpected partners for *Schumacher's Le Castellet*, a
classic Provençal floral-and-ribbon pattern, in writer
Elizabeth Mayhew's Millbrook, New York, home.

Window treatments in an antique-inspired floral add warmth to Sarah Brown's tightly edited dining room. OPPOSITE: Warm pink envelops the generously sized bathroom of designer Anna Haines's London house, where a curvy Bauhaus rope chair sits next to a clawfoot tub.

In a living room with all the elements of a classically formal space—upholstered walls, floral prints, skirted velvet sofas—Barrie Benson injected a dose of contemporary flair with a modern painting by Clare Rojas and fire engine–red trim. "The trim makes the room graphic and 'talks' to the art," the designer says. FOLLOWING PAGES, FROM LEFT: Hand-painted accents and primary colors take an antique bed and table in the Glebe House hotel in Devon, UK, decorated by Studio Alexandra, into the 21st century. An arresting apple painting inherited from her mother inspired this graphic pink-and-green color pairing in Amanda Lindroth's Palm Beach home. A vintage-feeling print covers the low-profile, clean-lined headboard of Octavia Dickinson's London bedroom.

Robin Henry covered an antique settee in an unexpected 1940s Josef Frank print for a result that feels decidely current but still rooted in the past.

Finishing Touches

We all know that Coco Chanel quote: "Before you leave the house, look in the mirror and take one thing off." With all due respect to Mlle. Chanel, we'd like to offer a bit of our own advice: When you get *back* to the house, keep on adding. If there's anything we've learned from the legendary decorators of yesteryear, its that the addition of a little something extra can turn a perfectly pretty room into a truly memorable one. Perhaps that means sewing a few yards of embroidered tape along the edge of a curtain, or swapping out the standard white lampshade for a block-printed silk one. Maybe it's upholstering a chair seat in custom needlepoint, or throwing an heirloom quilt over the foot of a bed. So go ahead and hang a tassel or tie on a bow: To quote another fashion legend, Iris Apfel, "More is more and less is a bore."

FROM THE ARCHIVES
OPPOSITE, CLOCKWISE FROM TOP LEFT: Albert Hadley filled his sister Betty Ann's home with family heirlooms. In a Manhattan living room by Mark Hampton, a gold satin ribbon was the literal bow on top. A ruffled lampshade and tapestry screen lent English charm to a Park Avenue apartment by Keith Irvine and Sam Blount of Irvine & Fleming. A needlepoint cushion adorned a gingham chair in decorator Michael Stanley's floral-filled house.

Caroline Gidiere went all out with contrast tape, cording and fringe on her lush living room sofa. OPPOSITE, CLOCKWISE FROM TOP LEFT: Barrie Benson used gutsy red tape to create a geometric frame for a classic mantlepiece. Unabashedly ornamental passementerie turns a pillow in *Gainsborough Velvet by Schumacher* into a work of art. Celerie Kemble added fringed skirts to a pair of cozy chairs in The Mayflower Inn. Jewelry designer Nicola Bathie McLaughlin, who knows a thing or two about proper embellishments, added *Schumacher's Valentin Silk Tassel* trim to bed curtains in *Barnet Cotton Check*; the wallcovering is *Chinois Palais by Mary McDonald for Schumacher*.

Petite shades offer a prime opportunity for extra adornment. CLOCKWISE FROM TOP LEFT: Ruthie Sommers embraces pattern-on-pattern pairings. Kate Aslangal of Oakley Moore Interior Design commissioned custom-painted shades from Sarah Blomfield that pull details from the wallcovering. Christian Ladd Interiors created pleated shades in *Dogwood Leaf by Miles Redd for Schumacher*. Simple raffia shades let *Spot and Star wallpaper by Molly Mahon for Schumacher* shine in a guest room by Studio Squire. OPPOSITE: A gathered floral shade makes breakfast in Philip Mitchell's kitchen nook a fanciful affair.

Libby Cameron channels the all-American nonchalance of her mentor Sister Parish in her own Maine summer house. OPPOSITE, CLOCKWISE FROM TOP LEFT: A needlepoint pillow, like this one in a cottage by Elizabeth Hay, is the epitome of vintage charm. Anthony Baratta designed this blue-and-white tapestry seat cushion for a French country feel. A playful contrast of old-fashioned florals and a cheeky saying greets overnight guests at Katie Rosenfeld's Massachusetts home. Technicolor hues make this custom bargello, stitched by Hunt & Hope, feel fresh.

A mismatched pair of heirloom quilts feels oh-so-right in coastal Maine, where Stefanie Scheer Young outfitted a guest room with an explosion of pattern and cozy textiles.

Don't be afraid to pair patterned bedding with an equally exuberant wallcovering. For her daughters' bedroom, CeCe Barfield Thompson chose a classic D. Porthault heart motif. OPPOSITE: A guest room at Christopher Spitzmiller's Clove Brook Farm, featuring *Garden Gate* and *Astor Braid* linens by Schumacher for Matouk, brings the outdoors in.

Antique tubs and sinks—or charming reproductions—make even a brand-new bath feel perfectly time-worn. CLOCKWISE FROM TOP LEFT: The rounded curves of a vintage-style tub complement the straight lines of checks and stripes on the floor and walls of Yasamin Feehily-Ghazizadeh's Victorian house. Lizzie Cullen Cox chose a generously sized clawfoot tub and serene *Fern Tree wallpaper by Schumacher* to create a relaxing retreat. *Citrus Garden wallpaper*, based on a 1947 design by Josef Frank, makes a whimiscal wainscoting for the original antique sink in Grace Mitchell's sunny powder room. Redouté floral prints hang above a vintage hand-painted basin in a country inn decorated by Studio Alexandra. OPPOSITE: "I like taking big, full-on traditional designs and giving them a modern tweak," says designer Samantha Todhunter, who used *Schumacher's Pyne Hollyhock* in the bathroom of her 1707 house. A scalloped mirror and lampshades play up a youthful angle.

ACKNOWLEDGMENTS

We would like to extend a heartfelt thank you to the following individuals, without whom this book would not have been possible:

Dara Caponigro for entrusting us with bringing this book to life. Thank you for your unwavering encouragement, support, and leadership throughout this process, and for sharing your wealth of knowledge along each step of the way. Your undying pursuit of beauty is an inspiration to us all. We couldn't have done it without you.

Lachlan Spence, Ella Charkes, Abigail Pratt, and Isabel Molster for your pivotal roles in gathering the images featured in this book and for the enthusiasm and positivity you brought to this project every day.

Timur Yumusaklar, F. Schumacher & Co.'s fearless leader who challenges us to forge our own path and open doors to new opportunities.

William Irvine for your copy editing skills and faultless attention to detail.

Alexandra Morris Flint for your deep knowledge of the design industry and your dedication to securing the archival images that were so crucial to this project.

Allie Johnson, artist extraordinaire, for your beautiful illustrations and for the joy that you brought to our collaboration.

Our FSCO Media editorial teammates—Tori Mellott, Eugenia Santiesteban Soto, and Hudson Moore—for their indispensable design knowledge and constant inspiration.

Jessica Tolmach for lending your support and expertise as we traveled together through uncharted territory.

The Schumacher Design Studio and our many collaborators for creating the beautiful product featured throughout this book. You are truly the best of the best.

Casey Saladino and Hannah Peters Siegfried for providing your much-needed assistance and legal expertise.

The talented community of designers from around the world whose incredible interiors never cease to amaze and delight us.

The visionary photographers whose mastery behind the lens brings these stunning projects to life.

The gracious homeowners featured in this book for inviting us inside your homes and allowing us to share them with the world.

The Hearst and Condé Nast photo departments for allowing us access to the breathtaking images produced by your storied magazines.

The entire F. Schumacher & Co. family for fostering a workplace filled with boundless creativity.

The Schumacher, Pozier, and Puschel families for your unmatchable stewardship of this company for more than 133 years.

The Schumacher Board of Directors—Lars Johansson, Tom Mendenhall, Andrew Puschel, Philip Puschel, Adam Schwartz and Alexa Wilson—for your dedication and stewardship of the Schumacher brand.

A note from Emma:
I couldn't be more grateful for my husband, Eric, for your love and support throughout this (oftentimes trying) process; to my mom, dad, stepmom, brother, and sister for your lifelong encouragement and for giving me the freedom to develop my own sense of self; to my loving grandparents for creating the homes that shaped the person I am today; to Joanna Saltz for believing that a peculiar interest in needlepoint and chintz was worth writing about; to Sophie Donelson for welcoming me into the world of design; to Dara Caponigro for your inspiring leadership; and, especially, to Steph Diaz for being the most patient and understanding collaborator I could ever have dreamed of working with—I appreciate you!

A note from Steph:
Thank you to my parents for always being there for me, for allowing me to pursue my love for design, and for never letting me give up. To my brother, thank you for challenging me to seek new heights every day. I am eternally thankful to Dara Caponigro for believing in me, supporting me, and always pushing me to make my work the best that it could possibly be. To my FSCO family and friends I've made along the way, thank you for making the last eight years such an incredible journey. And lastly thank you to Emma Bazilian for being the most wonderful partner. It was a true joy to get to work with you!

CHAPTER OPENERS

CHINTZ & FLORALS: *Salisbury Chintz fabric.* CHECKS & STRIPES: *Elton Cotton Check fabric.* TOILE: *Les Scenes Contemporaines wallpaper by Jill Lasersohn for Schumacher.* MATCHING: *Nancy fabric by Vogue Living for Schumacher.* SKIRTS: *Millicent wallpaper by Vogue Living for Schumacher.* SLIPCOVERS: *Floreana fabric.* BED HANGINGS: *Hydrangea fabric.* WINDOW TREATMENTS: *Les Fougeres fabric.* SCALLOPS: *Marella wallpaper by Vogue Living for Schumacher.* WICKER & RATTAN: *Ariana Floral Stripe fabric by Williamsburg for Schumacher.* TREILLAGE: *Zanzibar Trellis wallpaper.* DECORATIVE PAINTING: *Front Waltz wallpaper.* VINTAGE & ANTIQUES: *Blair Silk Epingle by Williamsburg for Schumacher.* COLLECTIONS: *Gerry Embroidery.* SETTING THE TABLE: *Le Citron wallpaper by Johnson Hartig/Libertine for Schumacher.* MAKING IT MODERN: *Magical Menagerie fabric.* FINISHING TOUCHES: *Caldwell Patchwork Chintz. All by Schumacher, fschumacher.com.*

PHOTOGRAPHY

William Abranowicz (P. 170) Melanie Acevedo (PP. 18, 82-83, 85, 87, 140, 159, 180, 203, 211, 213) Jean Allsopp (P.63) Brittany Ambridge (PP. 114-115) Michel Arnaud (PP. 37, 160) Alexandre Bailhache (P. 47) Chris Baker (PP. 25, 146, 147) Jan Baldwin/House Beautiful/Hearst Magazine Media, Inc. (P. 167) Allaire Bartel (P. 210) Anna Routh Barzin (P. 95) Roland Beaufre (P. 156) Jonathan Becker (P. 139) Tim Beddow (PP. 51, 71) Jane Beiles (P. 202) Fernando Bengoechea (PP. 198-199) Joakim Blockstrom (PP. 126-127) Jonathan Bond (PP. 242, 250) Antoine Bootz/House Beautiful/Hearst Magazine Media, Inc. (P. 75) Kelli Boyd (P. 189) Carmel Brantley (PP. 154-155) Brian Vanden Brink (P. 167) Simon Brown (PP. 84, 171) Max Burkhalter (PP. 64-65) Alun Callender (PP. 38-39) Darren Chung (P. 249) Patrick Cline for Lonny Magazine (P. 85) Paul Costello/OTTO (PP. 56-57, 77, 134) Billy Cunningham (P. 237) Billy Cunningham/House Beautiful/Hearst Magazine Media, Inc. (P. 101, 111) Jake Curtis (P. 92) Kip Dawkins (P. 249) Gabby Deeming (P. 174) Donna Dotan (P. 124) Timmy Dowling (P. 204) Courtesy of Dorothy Draper & Company Inc. (P. 31) Michael Dunne/House Beautiful/Hearst Magazine Media, Inc. (P. 75) Phillip Ennis (PP. 132-133) Pieter Estersohn (PP. 161, 162-163) Faulconer-Fenn/House Beautiful/Hearst Magazine Media, Inc. (P. 61) Richard Felber/House Beautiful/Hearst Magazine Media, Inc. (PP. 31, 91, 237) Finn Studio (PP. 230, 249) Miguel Flores-Vianna (PP. 9, 118-119) Scott Frances/OTTO (P. 7) Nicole Franzen (PP. 130-131) Douglas Friedman/Trunk Archive (P. 125) Oberto Gili (PP. 13, 32, 54) Laurey Glenn (PP. 2, 55, 146) Noa Griffel for Tory Burch (P. 215) Roger Guillemot/Connaissance des Arts/akg-images (P. 61) Natasha Habermann (P. 35) Hall (P. 153) John M. Hall, Courtesy of the Special Collections Research Center at North Carolina State University Libraries (P. 219) Nelson Hancock (P. 188) Heidi Harris (P. 85) David Hillegas (PP. 94, 185, 204, 238) Lizzie Himmel (PP. 167, 195) Emmie Hope (P. 242) Horst P Horst/Conde Nast/Shutterstock (PP. 7, 75, 139, 153, 195, 209) Horst P Horst/House and Garden/Conde Nast (PP. 7, 219) Laetitia Hussian (P. 198) Alexander James (P. 143) R.L. Johnson (P. 167) Stephen Kent Johnson (PP. 0, 36, 200-201) Stephen Karlisch (P. 168) Max Kim-Bee/OTTO (PP. 52, 53, 67, 157, 190-191, 202-203, 212, 239, 247) Ken Kirkwood (P. 219) Francesco Lagnese/OTTO (PP. 4, 16, 19, 20-21, 22-23, 70, 79, 85, 103, 114, 115, 116-117, 142, 148-149, 189, 223, 224-225, 228-229, 239, 240) Tom Leonard/Conde Nast/Shutterstock (PP. 13, 111) Nathalie Lété (P. 172) Sean Litchfield (P. 49) Thomas Loof (PP. 106, 184-185, 246) Steve Lovi/House Beautiful/Hearst Magazine Media, Inc. (P. 209) Spencer Lowell (P. 209) Peter Margonelli (P. 237) Nicolas Mathéus (P. 141) Aimée Mazzenga (P. 128) James McDonald (P. 102) Read McKendree (PP. 9, 14-15, 35, 80, 159, 204, 222-223, 242, 244-245) Lilse McKenna (P. 78) Nicola McLaughlin (P. 239) James Merrell (PP. 17, 126, 189, 243) Grace Mitchell (P. 249) Derry Moore/Conde Nast (P. 7) James Mortimer/House & Garden (P. 123) James Mortimer/World of Interiors (P. 111) Keith Scott Morton (P. 242) Michael Mundy (P. 111) Amy Neunsinger (PP. 40, 41, 80-81, 128, 144-145, 222) Peter Nyholm/Conde Nast/Shutterstock (P. 61) Peter Nyholm/House and Garden/Conde Nast Publications, Inc. (P. 61) David Parmiter (P. 31) David Phelps/House Beautiful/Hearst Magazine Media, Inc. (P. 101) Photography by Sotheby's (P. 195) Eric Piasecki (PP. 66, 146, 232-233) Karen Radkai (PP. 91, 179) Paul Raeside/OTTO (P. 33) Lilo Raymond/House Beautiful/Hearst Magazine Media, Inc. (P. 47) Laura Resen (PP. 13, 47, 50-51) JoAnna Robertson (P. 240) Jack Robinson/Hulton Archive/Getty Images (P. 31) Jo Rodgers (P. 205) Antoine Rozès (PP. 54-55) Lindsay Salazar (P. 158) Tim Salisbury (P. 93) Nikolas Sargent (PP. 112-113) Annie Schlechter (PP. 50, 104, 128, 173, 182-183, 184, 196, 197, 199, 241) Charles Schneider/Architectural Digest/Conde Nast Publications, Inc. (P. 123) Fritz von der Schulenburg (P. 179) Michael Sinclair (P. 128) Annie Sloan (P. 175) Walter Smalling/House Beautiful/Hearst Magazine Media, Inc. (P. 91) Chris Snook (PP. 43, 227) Angelica Squire (P. 240) Andrew Steel (P. 226) John Stewart/Conde Nast/Shutterstock (P. 153) Yuki Sugiura (PP. 86, 86-87, 105, 220-221) George R. Szanik/House Beautiful/Hearst Magazine Media, Inc. (P. 75) Alicia Taylor (PP. 62, 186-187) Astrid Templier (P. 34) Trevor Tondro (P. 9) Lesley Unruh (P. 9) Simon Upton (PP. 26-27, 35, 42, 76, 107, 129, 135) Jonny Valiant (PP. 169, 230-231) Peter Vitale (PP. 101, 237) William Waldron (PP. 35, 170-171, 179) Björn Wallander/OTTO (PP. 48, 181) Rachel Whiting (P. 231) Brian Woodcock (PP. 68-69, 81, 96-97, 214) Stephanie Woodmansee (P. 127)

COVER:
Garden Gate Chintz by Schumacher

ENDPAPERS:
Cabanon Stripe fabric by Schumacher

First published in the United States in 2022 by Schumacher Books
A division of FSCO MEDIA
459 Broadway
New York, NY 10013

Distributed by Monacelli
A Phaidon Company
65 Bleeker Street, 8th Floor
New York, NY 10012

Charm School: The Schumacher Guide to Traditional Decorating for Today
Copyright © 2022 Schumacher Books
Photography copyright © artists
Art directed and edited by Stephanie Diaz
Written and edited by Emma Bazilian
Publisher: FSCO MEDIA
Editorial Director: Dara Caponigro

Printed in Italy
2022 2023 2024 2025 2026 2027 / 10 9 8 7 6 5 4 3 2 1
ISBN: 978-1-58093-622-4
Library of Congress Control Number: 2022916496

Visit us online:
fschumacher.com
instagram.com/schumacher1889
youtube.com/schumacher1889
pinterest.com/schumacher1889